Shawn,

I Love You [barcode] ...

inch of my soul. You are with me in every thought I have every single day of my life. You have been a huge part of my life. You have helped me with so much. Know that I will be here to do the same for you clear through our old and gray years. While you take this journey in your life always always remember you have people at home that love you and are weighting with open arms and loving thoughts. Take Care of you always! Never ever be a hero Shawn! →

Just do your job. Do what you are there to do. And then get back here. Don't worry about any of us! We are going to be fine! I promise!

Brother know every day that I love you with such unconditional love!!!.

You are my world! Come home safe!

I love you!!.
Sis

a special gift for you

Sharon Franklin

with love,

Kim Franklin (sis)

date

10·4·04

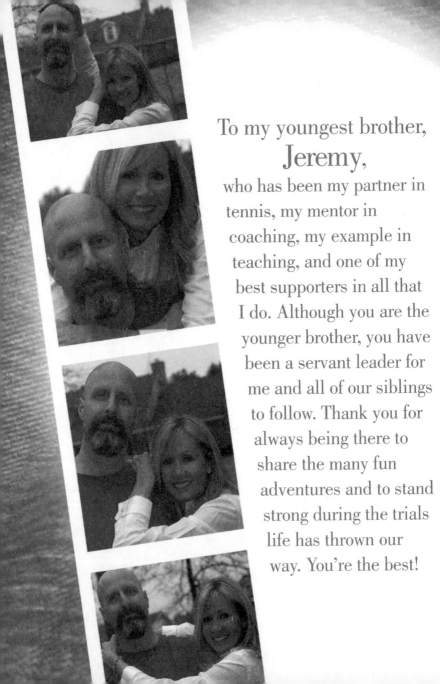

To my youngest brother,
Jeremy,
who has been my partner in tennis, my mentor in coaching, my example in teaching, and one of my best supporters in all that I do. Although you are the younger brother, you have been a servant leader for me and all of our siblings to follow. Thank you for always being there to share the many fun adventures and to stand strong during the trials life has thrown our way. You're the best!

Stories, sayings, and scriptures to Encourage and Inspire

hugs™
for
brothers

CHRYS HOWARD
Personalized Scriptures by
LEANN WEISS

Our purpose at Howard Publishing is to:

- *Increase faith* in the hearts of growing Christians
- *Inspire holiness* in the lives of believers
- *Instill hope* in the hearts of struggling people everywhere

Because He's coming again!

Hugs for Brothers © 2004 Chrys Howard
All rights reserved. Printed in the United States of America
Published by Howard Publishing Co., Inc.
3117 North 7th Street, West Monroe, LA 71291-2227
www.howardpublishing.com

04 05 06 07 08 09 10 11 12 13   10 9 8 7 6 5 4 3 2 1

Paraphrased scriptures © 2004 LeAnn Weiss, 3006 Brandywine Dr.
Orlando, FL 32806; 407-898-4410

Edited by Between the Lines
Interior design by Stephanie D. Walker
Photography by Chrys Howard and LinDee Loveland

Library of Congress Cataloging-in-Publication Data

Howard, Chrys, 1953–
    Hugs for brothers : stories, sayings, and scriptures to encourage and inspire / Chrys
  Howard ; personalized scriptures by LeAnn Weiss.
      p. cm.
    ISBN: 1-58229-372-4
      1. Christian men—Religious life. 2. Brothers—Religious life. I. Weiss, LeAnn. II. Title.

BV4528.2.H68 2004
242'.642—dc22   2004047495

Contents

a brother's love

My unfailing love surrounds the man who trusts in Me. I've lavished My love on you, calling you My child; now show love to others, even as I've shown love to you. When love is the trademark of your life, others will know you follow Me.

Loving you always,
Your Heavenly Father of Good and Perfect Gifts

—from Psalm 32:10; 1 John 3:1; John 15:12; 13:35

The dictionary definition of *love* is simple. It says love is "a fond attachment or a warm affection for another." For some reason that definition just doesn't seem to say enough.

The Bible says it best in 1 Corinthians 13. From being patient and kind to always protecting, trusting, and preserving, the challenge of loving others as God loves us is sometimes a daunting task. When you were a child, there were probably many days when you weren't as patient or kind as you should have been with your siblings. Perhaps you were easily angered or kept a few records of a brother's or sister's wrongdoing to share with your parents when it seemed convenient.

As a brother you may not often say "I love you" to your brothers or sisters. But there's never been any doubt that you do love them.

Love is what caused you to spend your hard-earned allowance on Christmas presents when you were a child and what still causes you to want to spend holidays with your family today. Family life is sustained by love, whether the words are spoken or not. Love is more about actions—steps taken by an incredible brother like you.

Love really is unexplainable. Webster couldn't adequately define it, and chances are you can't either. You just know your family is as important to you as you are to them.

Perhaps one definition of *love* is simply *a brother*.

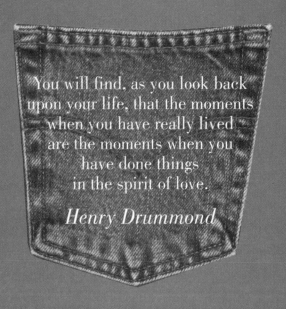

You will find, as you look back
upon your life, that the moments
when you have really lived
are the moments when you
have done things
in the spirit of love.

Henry Drummond

"Don't you forget who's responsible for those nice toys you like so well—the corner office, your fancy sports car, and that expensive condo. You blow this deal for me, and it'll cost you dearly!"

Love Is the Best Medicine

"Dear God, please let her be OK." Alone, Johnny Hutton prayed the words aloud as he drove to the hospital to see Mary. He was intent on getting there as quickly as possible, but his little sister's accident made him keenly aware of the danger he faced by driving too fast or allowing his emotions to distract him.

The ring of his cell phone startled him, making him jump. He felt his heart pounding—was it his imagination, or could he actually hear it beating? He reached to pull the phone from the breast pocket of his suit coat and was surprised to see his hand trembling. Was it his parents with more news about Mary—worse news? Suddenly, his mouth was as dry as cotton. He swallowed hard and wondered if he was capable of speaking.

"Hello?" Johnny sounded much calmer than he felt.

"Where are you?" the voice on the other end of the line roared. "The Gunderson meeting starts in ten minutes, and my key man is AWOL."

Johnny sucked in air and grimaced with sudden realization and discomfort.

"The meeting," Johnny croaked. "I forgot."

"It's the most important meeting of the year!" the voice bellowed. "How could you forget? You'd better have a good—"

"Mr. Potter," Johnny interrupted bluntly, his boldness fueled by anger at his boss's callousness and his own fear for Mary. "My sister has been in a car accident. I'm on my way to the hospital now."

Johnny felt Mr. Potter's shock in the awkward silence. Johnny offered no more explanation, distracted by the difficult job of trying to find a parking space along the crowded streets and parking lots near the hospital.

"Is it bad?" Potter asked, subdued.

"I don't know yet," Johnny said in a controlled tone. "No one in my family has seen her yet. We just know she's unconscious."

"Unconscious, eh?" the man said thoughtfully. "I don't suppose she'd know, then, if you didn't get there for another hour or two."

"Mr. Potter!" Johnny protested incredulously. "Even if *she* doesn't know, *I* know."

"Everything depends on this meeting," Johnny's boss stressed. "Come for just an hour. I know we can seal this deal in no time."

"No!" Johnny shouted with his jaw firmly set.

"Maybe we can delay them for an hour or two." Mr. Potter was scrambling. "You could get here by then, couldn't you?"

"Absolutely not," Johnny said emphatically. "My sister needs me. I don't know how long she'll need me, but as long as she does, I'll be at her side."

"Hutton!" Potter screamed into the phone. "Don't you forget who's responsible for those nice toys you like so well—the corner office, your fancy sports car, and that expensive condo. You blow this deal for me, and it'll cost you dearly!"

"Not as dearly as if I miss this time with my sister," Johnny said quietly with unmistakable resolve. He pulled into a tiny parking space just being vacated by a motor scooter. "Good-bye, Mr. Potter." He pushed the button to end the call and turned off his engine.

As he opened his car door, the phone rang again. Johnny imagined that the ring sounded angry. He knew who it would be.

He took a deep breath then pressed the off button, silencing the phone instantly. It felt dangerous but incredibly freeing.

Johnny raced up the sidewalk to the hospital. In a surreal moment of utter clarity, he noted that he'd taken a parking spot he never would have chosen under normal circumstances. It was far too narrow and exposed, flanked by beat-up old junkers parked haphazardly. Normally, he would have taken great care to protect his sleek black Porsche from dings and scratches, but now all that mattered was getting to Mary quickly.

The tight space by the front door was a godsend. Johnny breathed a quick prayer of thanks and hoped it was a good sign.

When Johnny found the waiting room, his anxious parents leaped up and ran to embrace him. "Oh, Johnny," his mother said, melting into Johnny's arms and burying her head in his chest. "I'm so glad you're here."

"Good of you to come, son," his father mumbled perfunctorily. "Hope you're not missing anything at work."

"Nothing important," Johnny said dryly. It shook him to see that even his usually stalwart father had been crying. "What's wrong?" he asked with growing alarm. "How is she?"

Johnny could feel his mother's body wracked with deep, silent sobs. "Is she—"

"We don't know anything yet," Johnny's dad said, pausing to bite his quivering lower lip. "She's still unconscious. Hit her head on the windshield. Wasn't going that fast, but wasn't wearing a seatbelt either." The words spilled out in uneven torrents. "No one can tell me how bad my little girl is."

Johnny put his arm around his dad's shoulder and pulled him close. The three of them stood that way for a long time, drawing strength from each other and supporting each other.

"Are you here for Mary Hutton?" The voice startled them, tearing them out of their mutual embrace.

"Yes, do you know how she is?" Johnny spoke for his shaken parents.

"I'm Dr. Brazil," the young man in hospital greens said, extending his hand first to Johnny, then to his father and mother. "I've given Mary a thorough examination," he began, looking down at his clipboard—whether to refresh his memory about Mary's condition or to escape the intense eye contact with his worried parents, Johnny wasn't sure.

"There's a lot we don't know," the doctor continued. "She has a nasty bump on her head and some swelling on her brain. We won't know the extent of her injury—whether there's brain damage—until she wakes up." He paused for a moment when Johnny's mother gasped in dismay.

"When will that be?" Johnny's dad asked, anguished.

"No one can tell," the doctor said kindly. "She may wake up in a few minutes and be perfectly fine."

"Or?" Johnny pressed.

"Or . . . it could take hours, weeks . . . maybe even a month or more. We just have to wait and see. Her brain needs a vacation, so to speak. She needs time to heal." Johnny's mother was sniffling loudly as the doctor tried to offer some hope. "She's a healthy young woman. Let's see what her body can do to bring her out of this."

"What can we do to help her, doctor?" Johnny asked, rubbing his hand reassuringly on his mother's back.

"Stay with her," the doctor encouraged them. "Talk to her. Sing to her. Do whatever it is your family does together. Let her know you're there for her."

"We can do that," Johnny said, determined that his sister would never be alone.

"Mommy!" six-year-old Mary screeched as Barbie flew over the seat into the back of the station wagon. "He's doing it again!"

"Johnny!" their mother said sternly. "Be nice to your sister."

"G.I. Joe is NOT Barbie's husband!" Nine-year-old Johnny

spat the words distastefully. "Tell her to stay on her side of the car and leave my things alone."

"It's a long trip," Dad piped up. "You should help keep your sister occupied instead of teasing and annoying her."

"But she ruins my toys," Johnny protested.

"It's just stuff," Mom said with a sigh. "Someday you'll learn that things aren't important, but your sister is."

"Enough!" Dad warned. "Can't you just sit quietly next to your sister for even a little while? Will you do that for me, please?"

"What, and ruin all my fun?"

"Johnny!" Mom scolded, exasperated.

"Johnny! Johnny, wake up."

"Huh?" He was no longer in the car with his sister but asleep in a chair by her bedside fifteen years later. He quickly turned to check on her—the bump had gone down and her color had returned, but she still lay motionless.

But this time, Mary was just sleeping. The night before, Mary had awoken from her four-day coma, weak but alert and intact. The family had been there to witness her awakening with joyful celebration. Then when she'd fallen asleep again—this time in normal, healthy slumber—Johnny had sent his parents home for some much-needed rest.

Now it was morning, and Johnny's mother had returned to relieve him. He groaned as he sat up and took the cup of coffee she offered. His neck was stiff and his back ached, but he felt better than he had in . . . in a long time.

"You haven't left for more than a few hours all week." His mother sounded concerned but pleased. "Last week you told me it was crucial for you to work extra hard at the office this week while they decide who they'll promote. Aren't you missing something important?"

Johnny shrugged. "Nothing important."

She patted him lovingly on the arm. "You've sat here with your sister long enough," she told him. "I'll stay with her. You go on home and take care of your own things now. Will you do that for me, please?"

"What?" Johnny balked good-naturedly. "And ruin all my fun?" He couldn't help but smile. *Guess I have learned to sit quietly next to my sister—and what's truly important in life.*

2

a brother's
protection

I am your refuge and your fortress. My faithfulness will always protect you. Therefore, don't fear anything. When you abide in Me, I'll command My angels to care for you and guard you in all of your ways.

Sheltering you,
Your Trustworthy Father

—from Psalm 91:1–11

From a young age, you were probably given the assignment of protecting your siblings. "Watch out for your sister!" "Don't let your brother out of your sight!" It's a heavy burden to place on a young boy, but you took the responsibility seriously, and more than once you saved your brother or sister from certain disaster.

Protector extraordinaire! That's you. Superman couldn't have done a better job. How many times you wanted to turn the other way and let your siblings try to make it without coming to their rescue. But you never did. That's because God placed you in the special role of being a brother. And one of the job descriptions of being a brother is being a protector.

You had many occasions to protect your brothers and sisters. Many times your parents or other adults asked you to guard them, help them, or just go check on them. But there were lots of other times when you just took it upon yourself to protect weaker brothers or sisters from bullies or strangers. You gladly helped your siblings learn the ropes and even enjoyed looking out for them. You felt a sense of obligation to stand guard and a sense of pride that you did your job well.

Maybe you're grown now, but you still feel protective. When your siblings need you, you're always there. So don't take your cape off yet; you're still on duty.

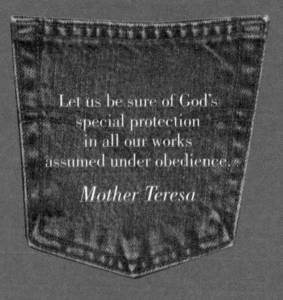

Let us be sure of God's
special protection
in all our works
assumed under obedience.

Mother Teresa

From their earliest years, Kerry had usually let Kevin call the shots. After all, Kevin was the one who thought of all those fun things to do—and actually had the courage to try them.

Out on a Limb

"Come on up," Kevin yelled to Kerry from the branch of the sweet-gum tree that hugged the fence in their new backyard. "You can see the school from up here. And there's Jimmy's house over on the next street!"

"I don't know," Kerry answered back. "Mom doesn't want us in that tree." Kerry was always concerned about their mother's feelings, while Kevin sometimes let the thrill of adventure cloud his thinking.

"Mom's not here," Kevin yelled down to his brother. "Dad's in charge, and he didn't say we couldn't." He climbed up a little higher. "I'm up here. You'll be OK."

a brother's protection

The twins were nine years old, and though they were best friends, they were far from identical. By a mere four and a half minutes, Kevin was older. With blond hair and mischievous blue eyes, he had all the makings of a real live Dennis the Menace. But Kerry had brown hair and eyes so dark they almost looked black. The differences didn't stop with their appearances; Kevin never met a stranger and enjoyed being the center of attention, while Kerry was shy and quiet.

From their earliest years, Kerry had usually let Kevin call the shots. After all, Kevin was the one who thought of all those fun things to do—and actually had the courage to try them. Kevin dreamed of forts in the woods and go-carts made from leftover parts around the house. Kerry was just glad Kevin always included him in his adventures.

"Think before you do something," their mother often said when Kevin came home with a new cut, scrape, or bump. "If I've told you once, I've told you a million times, you're going to hurt yourself someday—or Kerry. I declare, a special angel must be watching over you!"

But Kevin would never dream of putting Kerry in any real danger. He viewed himself as Kerry's protector. He stood up for Kerry when kids at school teased him for not talking to them. He always made sure the other boys included Kerry in their games of marbles or basketball at recess. Kevin and Kerry had grown to trust each other completely.

"OK, here I come." Kerry finally gave in to his brother's urgings.

"Just don't blame me if Mom finds out and gets mad at us. Remember, this wasn't my idea!"

"Relax." Kevin blew off Kerry's caution. "I know what I'm doing. Nothing's gonna happen."

Kerry started to climb. It was easy. It was fun. Kevin was right—it was exhilarating. Branch by branch, Kerry inched his way higher toward Kevin. Soon the limbs were only about four inches around. Kerry stopped moving and twisted his face into a humorous look of uncertainty, his eyes wide as the branches shook and leaves fell to the ground. Kerry chose places for his feet and hands with even greater care.

a brother's protection

"You've almost made it!" Kevin shouted encouragement to keep his brother climbing. "You can do it. Keep going."

"Grab my hand," Kevin said as Kerry reached the last branch that would put him on the limb just below.

"You did it, Kerry. Isn't this neat?" Kevin's blue eyes twinkled with excitement, adrenaline, and the thrill of having conquered something bigger than himself. The tree was higher than either boy thought it would be, but once they were there, it was well worth the effort. They were part of the sky. For a few minutes, they felt the freedom a bird must feel perched on a limb of a tree. The breeze played roughly through their hair. They could see for a mile! They smiled at each other, proud of their accomplishment.

"Look how far you can see," Kerry said, enthralled by the view.

"Wouldn't it be fun if Mom let us build a tree house up here?" Kevin practically squealed at the thought.

"This is pretty cool," Kerry admitted with a reluctant smile. "But this tree really isn't big enough for a tree house. It's barely holding us!" Kerry looked at the branch beneath them and the ground far below. "C'mon," he urged. "The sooner we get down, the better." He carefully positioned one of his feet on the limb below and bounced a few times to test its strength.

"But we just got up here," Kevin protested. "I like being here. Let's stay a while longer."

"I don't think it's very safe," Kerry pressed.

"It'll be fine," Kevin promised. "Relax and enjoy the view. See that big dog on the next block? Oh, and look at that great motorcycle over there."

"Wow," Kerry agreed. "You really can see a lot from up here. Like down the street, I see . . . MOM!"

"Mom! Yikes. Guess you're right. It's time to get down."

Kerry turned his body to begin climbing down from the tree.

"Come on, Kerry, hurry. We've got to get down before she catches us."

"I'm hurrying. Don't rush me. We don't want to fall."

"You're too slow, Kerry. Look out, let me go first."

"No, Kevin. Wait! The branch won't hold us both!"

But Kevin didn't listen—or wait. He pushed onto the small limb next to his brother. Instinctively, Kerry grabbed the trunk of the tree and held on for dear life. In a fraction of a second, both boys heard a loud *crack!* The branch beneath their feet gave way, dropping Kevin instantly through branch after branch and finally spilling him onto the ground—hard.

"Ooooph." Kevin made the sound involuntarily as the air was knocked from his lungs. For a moment he couldn't make another sound. But soon he was crying in agony and holding his arm.

Kerry lowered himself to another branch, then energized by his brother's cries, he quickly swung down another few feet before leaping from the tree and landing at Kevin's side.

"Hold on, Kevin," he urged. "I'll get help!"

Kerry ran faster than he'd ever run before. In five seconds flat, he was around the front of the house and alongside his mother's car as she pulled into the driveway.

"Mom, come quick!" Kerry yelled. "Kevin's hurt. It's his arm. I think it's bad."

With surprising calmness, the boys' mom ran to the backyard. He could tell she was worried though, because she ran so fast Kerry couldn't keep up with her.

She examined Kevin closely, comforting him and kissing his forehead. "I think it's broken," she announced. "We'll have to get you to the doctor and get you in a cast."

"A cast?" Kevin asked, intrigued. "Cool!"

"Hmm." Their mother frowned suspiciously, analyzing the fallen leaves and broken branch on the ground. "By any chance did you disobey me and climb that little tree?" she grilled Kevin sternly.

He didn't answer, but for Kevin, not denying something was about as close as he got to admitting it. "You could have been killed," she continued. "Can't you see this tree is too small to climb safely? It's branches are too thin to hold a big boy like you."

Neither twin spoke. What was there to say? They were caught red-handed. Punishment was sure to follow.

"You know there are consequences to disobedience. Your father and I will decide later how to punish you." She shook her head and helped Kevin get to his feet, cradling his broken arm gently. "And aren't you glad Kerry didn't follow your crazy lead and climb up there with you? The tree never would have supported the weight of both you boys."

a brother's protection

Both boys froze. She didn't know. She thought only Kevin had disobeyed. Kerry was home free.

Kerry started to open his mouth to correct her, but Kevin's protective instincts kicked in. "That's right, Mom," he said loudly, drowning out Kerry and willing him with his eyes to be quiet. "Kerry warned me not to climb the tree, but I wouldn't listen. I'm just glad I didn't land on top of him when I hit the ground."

Kerry took a deep breath, then plunged right in. "Kevin's just trying to protect me," he admitted. "I knew it was wrong to climb the tree, but I did it anyway. I climbed the tree too. I deserve to be punished along with Kevin."

Kevin's eyes bugged out, surprised. "It's not his fault, Mom. I made him do it."

"You didn't make me," Kerry countered. "I did it because I wanted to. Kevin always has such exciting ideas and a cool way of looking at things. I want to see things the way he does—even if just for a moment before we come crashing down. The view, Mom—it was awesome!"

"I know what you mean," his mother responded with a sympathetic smile. "I wish you could see what I see—two special brothers who love each other very much and will do whatever they can to protect each other."

Kevin and Kerry looked at each other sheepishly and smiled. Sure, they learned important things that day about the consequences of disobedience—and about how much weight a sweet gum tree will support. But most importantly, they learned something about themselves as brothers— broken arm and all.

3

a brother's example

I modeled a lifestyle of servant-hood. Likewise, may you set an example for others in what you say, how you live and love, and the level of your faith and purity. Do what is good!

Your Example,
Jesus

—from John 13:15; 1 Timothy 4:12; Titus 2:7

As a brother, your siblings have always looked to you to see how you would behave in a given situation. Whether you like it or not, you're their example. "Be careful what you say and do," your father probably said. "Others are watching you." Your father's words have held true many times in the course of your life.

While it might have been much easier to do your own thing and live only for yourself, you just couldn't do it. From your earliest memories of being a brother, you knew someone was looking up to you. Whether it was to watch how you handled yourself on the basketball court or to listen as you interacted with friends, your words and actions affected others.

Being an example is a hard job, but it comes with great rewards. Remember the first time you noticed your little brother trying to walk or talk like you? You were proud to have influenced him positively. Remember that card you received from your sister, thanking you for being the example she needed throughout her high-school years? You were relieved to know she had seen the good in you.

Yes, it's tough to live your life with someone always watching, but you were—and still are— up to the challenge. You have a job to do, through your example at school, at work, and in life—being the best brother you can possibly be.

The ultimate measure
of a man is not where he stands
in moments of comfort and
convenience, but where
he stands at times of
challenge and controversy.

Martin Luther King Jr.

Jamie passed Andy early on, amused that
his strength seemed to have sputtered
since the day before. Serves him right
for being a big shot yesterday.

The View from Higher Up

"This trip will be a disaster if *he* goes," sixteen-year-old Jamie Taylor complained to her mother when her little brother Andy first spoke of going on the trip. The Wilderness Trek was an annual high-school-only trip designed to bring the youth-group members closer together and help them know themselves and God better. It was something every kid in the church waited for eagerly. But Jamie would be the only person with the misfortune of having her little brother along.

"It'll be good for you both," Jamie's mom said. "Maybe you'll learn to get along when you have to."

a brother's example

Andy was just seventeen months younger than Jamie, but it might as well have been five years for all the distance between them. Andy was so immature. She wished she had an older brother like her friend Candace did. Candace's older brother was interesting and mature. The only word that described her own brother was *annoying*.

"Andy will just bug me, and I'll come back hating him even more!" Jamie groaned, exasperated. "He'll drive my friends crazy too. It'll ruin everything. Please don't let him go."

"Jamie, I'm not going to let you ruin a perfectly good trip for your brother. He's going, and that's final!"

The bus ride to Colorado wasn't as bad as Jamie had anticipated. Andy sat in the back while she chose a seat up front. With her earphones in, she hardly noticed him.

"Hey," Jamie felt someone tapping her on the shoulder. She took the earphones out to hear what her friend Lindsay was saying. "Your brother's funny!"

"Funny?" Jamie replied, puzzled. *Funny looking . . . funny smelling . . .*

"I didn't know he could imitate people like that." Lindsay seemed genuinely impressed. "He sounded just like

Pastor Dan. Did you hear him? And he knows the words to every song on the radio. Have you heard him sing? I bet you guys have so much fun at home."

Yeah, right. Jamie put her earphones back in. The truth was she hadn't heard him sing or do imitations, and she really didn't care to. But it bothered her that Lindsay could see something in her brother that she couldn't. *Is he really funny?* she mused, looking up from her book. *Have I just not listened?* She heard laughter coming from the back of the bus and toyed with the idea of going back there but decided she didn't want to watch her brother make a fool of himself. She went back to reading, trying to ignore the laughter.

"Jamie, did you bring an extra fork?" Andy asked when they arrived at the little town in Colorado to begin their adventure. The group would spend the first night outdoors before climbing the mountain, so they could get acclimated to the higher altitude. It would also let the campers try out their equipment to make sure they had everything they would need.

"I can't believe it, Andy." Jamie shook her head and looked disgusted. "Why didn't you come prepared? You had the list just like the rest of us did."

"I have an extra one you can have," Candace offered.

"Thanks." Andy smiled gratefully at his sister's friend.

"I don't know why you're so hard on Andy," Candace chided Jamie later. "He's kinda cute." Jamie just rolled her eyes as Candace turned away with one final rebuke: "I wouldn't mind having a brother like Andy."

The next morning the eager teens filled their water bottles, tied matching bandannas around their heads, and helped each other strap on their backpacks. They were ready to conquer the mountain. They had been told it would be a tough day with six hours of walking. *Tough* was an understatement. They quickly learned how torturous it was to walk uphill while breathing thinner air with thirty to fifty extra pounds on their backs.

Jamie noticed that Andy was always in the front of the group, leading the pack. *Show off*, she thought as she saw him helping another hiker over a tree that was blocking the path. *He never helps me like that!*

That night at the campfire, Jamie's ears perked up as she heard Andy take a turn leading a song. She pretended to be drawing in the dirt beside her, but she was intently focused on her younger brother and the talent she was noticing in him for the first time. "Make me new, Lord Jesus, Make me new . . ." were the words to the song Andy chose. After devotions she wanted to tell him he'd done a good job, but she decided he didn't need any more attention. After all, he had three girls around him most of the night. *He'll just get a big head,* she reasoned.

The second day of the journey started out much like the first—crisp morning, beautiful vistas, and a long day of body-punishing exercise. But instead of leading the way as he had yesterday, Andy dropped to the very end, quickly outpaced by everyone except Randy, the youth pastor, who was laboring to climb.

Jamie passed Andy early on, amused that his strength seemed to have sputtered since the day before. *Serves him right for being a big shot yesterday.* "If you can't keep up, we'll leave you behind," she said as she breezed past him.

"Wait, Jamie." There was a hint of a plea in Andy's voice. "Please walk back here with me."

Something about his tone made her hesitate. She

paused, considering turning around or waiting for him to catch up, but years of conditioning won out. She started climbing again, throwing the words over her shoulder without turning. "I don't want to walk with you. Maybe you should have stayed home."

No more than ten minutes had passed when Jamie heard Andy shouting. "Hey, wait up!"

He's just trying to get attention, Jamie thought. But her annoyance turned to fear when Andy hollered, "Get the nurse. Bring help!"

What was wrong? Jamie's mind raced as fast as her heart. Had he broken something? Been bitten by a snake? Was he in danger of plunging down the mountain? "We've got trouble back here," Jamie relayed the message up the mountain, then turned and scrambled to get to Andy.

When she rounded the bend in the trail, she could see Andy struggling to remove his backpack while trying to support the youth pastor. As she got closer, she could see that Randy was perspiring heavily and gasping for air. He groaned miserably then doubled over, vomiting. Andy was keeping Randy from falling while trying to lower him gently to the ground. He spoke soothingly, "It'll be OK. Help's on the way, and God's here with us now."

"Oh, Andy," Jamie's voice quavered in fear. "What's wrong? Is he having a heart attack?"

She could tell by Andy's shrug that he didn't know, but his eyes clearly warned her not to scare Randy. She scanned the trail nervously. Where was the nurse? A few more students had gathered around by then. They all just stood and watched somberly. A few cried. Some mouthed silent prayers.

After what seemed like forever, the nurse was there. He felt Randy's forehead and took his pulse. The worried teens helped each other take off their backpacks and then sat in small groups, comforting and reassuring one other. Andy drew the anxious teens into a circle and prayed for their leader.

"We should take him down right away," the nurse told the first guide to reach the scene. "Moderate AMS."

The guide nodded knowingly.

"What's AMS?" Jamie asked. "Is it bad?"

"Acute Mountain Sickness," the young woman

explained. "His body didn't have time to adapt to the higher altitude. He'll be fine in a few days, but he's got to go lower."

"I guess that's the end then," Lindsay said bleakly. "We won't make it to the top after all."

"Why not?" Andy challenged, stepping forward.

Surprised, Jamie just stared at her little brother.

"Because our leader is sick," a boy named Peter responded. "It'll take at least two people to get him down the mountain."

"It's been so difficult already," Candace added. "We're all exhausted and sore. And could we all get altitude sickness too?" Murmurs of concern and agreement spread through the group.

Andy spoke firmly. "Randy can't take us to the top of the mountain as he planned. But you know he wanted us to make it. He hoped we'd learn to work together as a team and to persevere in the face of difficulty. We still have one guide, and some of us are adults."

The group considered Andy's words as he continued in low, earnest tones. "We've all struggled on this trip. We're all tired. We're worried about Randy and maybe a little scared. It's hard climbing a mountain. Tomorrow will be harder. But if we all stick together, we can do this—for each other and for Randy. Are you with me?"

Silence. Jamie studied her younger brother's face. She looked around at the small group of students dressed in sweatshirts and dirty jeans, far away from their usual world of makeup and name-brand clothes. Some were wiping tears from their eyes; all were holding on to friends for strength.

She walked over and stood beside her brother. She put her arm around him and with a shaky voice began to speak. "Most of you know that sometimes my brother and I don't get along." She paused, then smiled. "OK, so I hardly ever get along with my brother. But this morning in my quiet time, my Bible fell open to Proverbs 20:29. It says, 'The glory of young men is their strength.'"

Jamie started to cry. "I'm proud of Andy. His leadership and strength have been an inspiration to me this week. If he thinks we can still make it to the top of the mountain, I do too. I say let's go for it. What about you?"

a brother's example

Some nodded their heads; others smiled. Most pressed in around Jamie and Andy, shouting their agreement. "We're with you." "Let's stick together." "We can do this!"

Jamie hugged Andy and whispered so only he could hear. "I'm so glad you came on this trip. If you don't mind, I want to walk right beside you until we reach the top of the mountain."

4

a brother's
friendship

I've called you My friend and chosen you to make a difference spreading My love to those around you. Experience the up-lifting power of friendship. Two are better than one! If one falls down, your friend is there to help you up.

Eternally,
Your Friend and King

—from John 15:15–17; Ecclesiastes 4:9–10

"Friends are friends forever." The words to the song made famous by Michael W. Smith are especially true when it comes to the enduring relationships forged between brothers and sisters. Even as you fought over whose turn it was to sit in the front seat or who had to help set the table, there was never any doubt in your mind that you would be friends for life.

A friend is someone you can always turn to. Someone who knows you and loves you unconditionally. As a brother in our family, you are that person. You're always there to lend a hand or speak a word of encouragement. Your siblings will encounter many people, but as the brother, you will always hold a special place as one of the first and most influential men in their lives. You were the one they wanted to ride bikes with—who they wanted to throw a ball to. Together you ganged up on your parents, sold lemonade, and washed the dog in the bathtub. Together you rode roller coasters, made homemade valentines, and dreamed of building the greatest fort ever. When all the other kids in the neighborhood went home, you stayed.

Your mother told you to be nice to your siblings because they'll always be a part of you, and it's true. You are forever friends. Nothing can change or undo that— not time, distance, difficulties— not even death. A brother is forever.

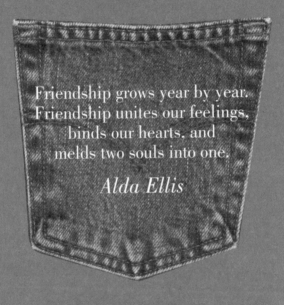

Friendship grows year by year.
Friendship unites our feelings,
binds our hearts, and
melds two souls into one.

Alda Ellis

They were the popular boys in high school

not just because they were good looking

and funny but also because

they had a genuine

friendship and respect for each other.

Stuck

"Remember how loud those sirens were?" Daryl laughed heartily and hit his younger brother on the arm. He was reclining in the same worn-out green lounger in which he used to watch his grandfather sleep during football games on Sunday afternoons. He tucked one arm securely behind his head as a makeshift pillow; the other arm was free to nudge his brother at appropriate times during their storytelling.

Marc pretended to be hurt where his brother had jabbed him. "Of course I remember," he responded with a roll of his eyes. "After all, I was the one stuck there. I wasn't going anywhere, but you were running around screaming like a maniac!"

The brothers were enjoying a family reunion at their grandparents' home. The talk had naturally turned to favorite childhood moments, and the house was alive with laughter . . . and with love. Grandparents, aunts, uncles, and cousins sat around the room and listened to the boyhood escapades of these two men as if they were watching comedians perform on the *Late Show with David Letterman*.

Now grown and living on opposite coasts, the brothers never let time or distance keep them apart for long. Daryl, a policeman in Los Angeles, and Marc, a pilot based in Atlanta, made sure they met four or five times a year for a hunting trip, a football game, or just a weekend of goofing off, reminiscing, and enjoying each other's company. The minute they would reunite, it was as if they were still living together and sharing daily adventures. They never lacked for something to talk about.

Daryl, six feet tall with his once-blond hair shaved close to his head, was older by two years. His "little" brother, Marc, was two inches taller than Daryl and, at thirty-eight, was beginning to have a few gray hairs sprinkled into his full head of black hair. Both were gifted with pleasing personalities that often made them the center of attention. They were the popular boys in high school and college—not just because they were good looking and funny but also because they had a genuine friendship and respect for each other. Even as little kids, they loved being together. They always looked out for each other. Daryl especially, as the older brother, looked out for Marc—but not on the day more than thirty years earlier that was now the subject of their banter.

"You were supposed to look after me," Marc said to Daryl, faking a pout like a five-year-old who'd lost his sucker. "You always had before."

"I *was* looking out for you," Daryl joked. "I thought you needed to learn a lesson. You did learn something, didn't you?" Daryl pressed his brother. "That's what true friends do for each other."

"Oh, I learned something all right." Marc feigned indignation. "I learned not to ask my big brother for help! With friends like you, who needs enemies?" It was Marc's turn to hit Daryl on the arm.

"No, really you learned not to put things where they don't belong," Daryl corrected. "Now that's a valuable lesson, don't you think?" He held up his hands to block the punch coming his way.

"OK, someone tell the whole story," Sarah, one of their cousins, urged.

"I'll tell it—it happened to me," Marc began. "We were at the Guyess Air Force base in Abilene, Texas, where Dad was stationed. I was about five, so Daryl must have been seven. Every afternoon we would play at the base playground. Remember the old metal slides? Well, I was climbing up the slide ladder when my finger accidentally went in a hole in the iron step."

"Accidentally!" Daryl shouted. "That was no accident; you did it on purpose. You never could stand to see something and not explore all the possibilities. I saved you from more disasters that would have resulted from your curiosity!" Daryl shook his head as he remembered additional, unspoken-of adventures that had landed Marc in a bind.

"Whatever!" Marc said, obviously enjoying himself. "So my finger went in the hole so easily, I never thought it would be so hard to pull it out. But the harder I tried, the more stuck I got."

"That's when he decided he needed his big brother to help him get out," Daryl said with mock contempt.

"Hey, I was only five, and I was stuck in a slide. What did you expect?"

Marc turned back to the cluster of relatives all caught up in laughter. "As I was saying, I was really stuck. So, of course, I called for Daryl to come and help me. But all he did was laugh. So I called for my friend Tommy. He started to go for help, but Daryl knocked him to the ground. He told him not to help me—that I would have to get out of the mess myself!"

"Wait a minute," Daryl interrupted, laughing. "It's time you all hear the rest of the story. Before he got his finger stuck, my sweet, innocent brother had been running through the house—which I warned him not to do—and he broke the special green vase Dad had brought Mom from Japan. *That's* the reason we were outside to begin with. Mom punished us *both* by banning us from the house for the afternoon."

a brother's *friendship*

"Is that what happened, Daryl?" the boys' mother, Claire, broke in, surprised. "It was so unlike you to not help Marc, but I didn't know until today that you were paying him back for getting you in trouble."

Sarah spoke up again. "Finish the story," she urged. "Why isn't Marc still hanging from a slide in Texas?"

"Basically," Marc explained, "Daryl couldn't tackle all of our friends at once. Jamie Thomas escaped to get help."

"You should have seen the moms go into action." Daryl laughed as he described the scene. "They had grease and oil and peanut butter . . . anything they thought might slide Marc's chubby—and by then swollen—little finger out of the hole. But that finger was not coming out!"

"It's pretty funny now," Claire admitted, "but when I heard Daryl was fighting kids who were trying to get help for Marc, I wanted to hang *him* from the slide!"

Everyone in the room burst into laughter. "Like Daryl said," Claire continued, "we tried every home remedy we could think of, but nothing worked. We finally gave up and called the base police. Soon there were fire trucks, policemen, and even an ambulance rushing in to help free Marc.

Judging from the number of rescue workers who showed up, you would have thought the entire base was under attack."

"They finally had to get some metal cutters and cut me free from the slide," Marc said.

"I guess if it were up to Daryl, you'd still be hanging there." Claire chuckled and shook her head as she replayed the scene in her mind.

"Mom, you have to admit it was exciting," Daryl said, trying to justify his actions as a child. "They even wrote it up in the base newspaper. The headlines read 'Boy Rescued from Slide.' We were pretty famous for one day around there." Daryl got out of his chair and gave his mother a hug. "I really am sorry I gave you such a scare, Mom. I would have gotten help eventually," he assured her. "I just wanted Marc to think about his situation and why he was stuck. I took my job as a big brother seriously."

His mother smiled, unconvinced but benevolent.

"You know I was his best friend," Daryl said seriously. "I wouldn't have let him hang there forever."

Marc jumped out of his chair to join the two. "Do I get an apology now too? After all these years, it would do me good. I've probably got some deep-seated bruise to my psyche from the trauma of not being able to count on my big brother," he said with mock seriousness while opening his arms wide in an exaggerated invitation for a brotherly hug.

But Daryl's hug quickly turned into a wrestling match as the adult brothers seemed to become five and seven once again.

"You know you can count on me, brother," Daryl whispered so only his brother could hear as their relatives moved away to avoid being caught up in the scuffle. And the squeeze he got in return as they wrestled let him know that Marc knew.

5

a brother's strength

Share each other's burdens when life gets tough. Remember, no matter what you are facing, My joy is your strength. You don't have to be afraid, for I'm with you. I'll strengthen you and help you, upholding you with My righteous, powerful hand. I'm the strength of your heart and your portion forever! I'll show you the pathway to life.

Joyfully,
Your God

—from Galatians 6:2; Nehemiah 8:10; Isaiah 41:10; Psalms 73:26; 16:11

How many times did your mother tell you to take it easy? She worried that you wouldn't realize how strong you were and might harm your sister during a simple game of touch football. But actually, you did know. You realized you were strong way before you let on. That's the fun part of being a boy, isn't it? If you're the oldest, you always had a physical advantage; but even if your sister is older than you, you knew in your heart that one day you'd be bigger and stronger.

Remember when the tide turned? One day you were the scrawny little brother, and the next she was asking you to open jars and carry suitcases. In fact, your parents began asking you to do grown-up jobs too. Like mow the yard and rake the leaves. "Wait a minute!" you wanted to yell. "I'm just a kid!" But you weren't anymore.

People started to depend on your strength. Now you get to help carry a piano when your sister moves—for the third time—or help your brother build a deck. That's what a great brother like you does willingly! He lends a strong arm when needed.

But it's not just your physical strength they depend on; it's your inner strength as well. Your ability to stand strong in the midst of upheaval is important to your family. You're the kind of man they know they can count on, the kind of brother that brings the strength of love.

Simple pleasures of growing up together are preserved in the keepsake albums of our hearts.

Jane Debord

"Marvin, you don't have to do anything right now," Claudia told him, remembering advice she'd gotten when her husband died. "I'll be there tomorrow, and we'll get through this together."

Changing Seasons

They sat on the park bench like two old pigeons waiting for someone to feed them. Gold and brown leaves fell around them, and they watched as a soft breeze gently placed each leaf on the ground. He wore a hat to ensure warmth for his bald head. She tightened the scarf around her neck to block the cool breeze from her tender neck. It was a comfortable day for both of them. They were in a comfortable spot in life.

"Penny for your thoughts," Marvin said as he tossed a bit of bread to a hungry bird nipping at his worn walking shoes.

"Oh, I don't know," Claudia sighed. "I was just thinking how funny life is. We go out almost the same way we came in."

"Now don't get philosophical," Marvin said. "This is supposed to be our fun day."

Claudia shook her head and ran her fingers through her short gray hair. She placed a hand on her brother's arm. "Just think, here we are at the same park Mother used to take us to when we were kids. Remember how we fed the ducks in that pond and how Mother would make me share my bread with you because you always threw yours out too quickly?" Claudia smiled at the memory.

"You're right," Marvin responded. "We've both had interesting life journeys and are back to the same beginning." He peered over his glasses, seeming to look beyond the pond and into the past.

It had been three years since his wife, June, had died of a sudden heart attack. After fifty-five years of marriage, the thought of living in their home without her was more than he could bear. So after the funeral, when his sister had invited him to stay with her awhile, he'd been happy to accept. Claudia had lost her husband, Jack, many years earlier. Marvin had grieved with her, but only since the death of his own wife had he truly appreciated how strong his sister had been to make it alone.

As usual, Claudia had handled it as he expected his strong, older sister to—she had stayed tough, choosing to remain in her home alone. She'd had her job to keep her busy each day, and her daughter and three grandkids had lived close by. Marvin had faithfully called his sister every Sunday afternoon to check up on her. Once Claudia and Marvin had retired and the grandkids had gone to college, the sister and brother had spent even more time visiting each other.

Twenty years had passed since Jack's funeral. Then one week Marvin hadn't waited until Sunday to call.

"Claudia, she's gone." He had choked on the words.

"What are you talking about?" Claudia had asked, stunned.

"June's gone," Marvin had sobbed. "She had a heart attack last night."

"Oh, Marvin . . . I'm so sorry. I just can't believe it. June seemed so vital and alive."

Marvin had agreed. "She was only seventy-three."

"That's young these days!"

"We were going on a cruise this summer. We'd made all the plans." He had felt grief-stricken, lost. "Now what will I do?"

"Marvin, you don't have to do anything right now," Claudia had told him, echoing advice she'd gotten when her husband died. "I'll be there tomorrow, and we'll get through this together."

"I don't mean to worry you." Marvin had tried to sound strong.

"Marvin, I'm your big sister, and I always will be. It's my job to worry about you. I love you, and I'll see you tomorrow."

After the funeral Claudia had convinced Marvin to come to her house just for a visit. "You don't need to go back to your house right now. Come with me, and we'll go back in a few months and tackle the job of cleaning out June's things. You don't want to make any decisions right now anyway. You need time to heal."

So it had all started with a visit. Six months after June's death, Claudia had persuaded Marvin to move back to the little Arkansas town where they'd been raised. More than fifty years after setting out on their own, brother and sister again lived under the same roof.

They settled into a way of life reserved for seniors. Sunday was church, of course. Monday night was bridge at the senior center. Claudia's hair appointment was always on Tuesday, so Marvin took that day to work on his golf game. They loved Wednesday because Claudia cooked a big meal, and any family in town was welcome to come for supper before the midweek church service.

After company on Wednesday, Thursday was house-cleaning day. Marvin always did the dishes and the vacuuming. On many occasions Claudia commented that he had become a much better worker than she would have guessed when they were children.

On Friday Marvin and Claudia volunteered at their church, folding bulletins for Sunday. Saturday was their fun day. They took turns deciding what they would do. It was a comfortable life. They missed their spouses, but they enjoyed life together.

"Come on, let's walk over to that pond," Claudia said. It

was her day to choose their fun activity, and she had chosen to stroll in the park and enjoy the changing seasons.

"Marvin, remember that movie *Forrest Gump*, when his mother tells him 'life is like a box of chocolates'?"

"I remember." Marvin tossed a rock into the pond. "'You never know what you're gonna get.'"

Claudia nodded and smiled. "Well, I was looking at the autumn leaves, and I decided life is more like the changing seasons. You really *do* know what you're going to get. Think about spring with its fresh face like a newborn baby, ready for anything. And summertime, with it's hot, long days. It mirrors the impatience of youth—trying to accomplish all it can in one day. Then comes fall: the leaves change colors, and the days are shorter." She laughed and touched her hair. "Well, our hair certainly has changed colors, and we're ready to slow down and live shorter days.

"Now nature is preparing for winter, and you and I are as well. Our hair is the color of snow, and just like people do in the winter months, we've slowed down. During the winter people talk about what they did in the spring and summer.

In *our* winter years, we reflect on what we did in the earlier seasons of our lives."

Thoughtful, Marvin bent over to pick up another rock. He tossed it, making it skip across the smooth water four times before sinking. "Where did the years go, Claudia? I look at that swing over there and still see you pushing me while I'm shouting, 'Higher, higher!'" He chuckled at the warm memory. "You were a good big sister, Claudia. I've never said this to you, but I want you to know how much I appreciate your taking care of me these past three years. I couldn't have made it without you."

"No," Claudia broke in, tears moistening her eyes. "I couldn't have made it without you, Marvin. I know it seems that I was still being the big sister when I asked you to move in with me, but actually I couldn't stand to face winter alone. I was your big sister, always looking out for you, ready to fight anyone who messed with you. But now you look after me too. When you moved in, you gave me back my spring and my summer. You've helped me embrace the autumn and given me courage to face the coming winter.

You chased away the loneliness and filled my life with love and friendship. You've eased my burden of caring for the house, the car, and everything else. You know, I'm not as strong as I used to be."

For the first time, Marvin saw Claudia without the filter of the take-charge, indestructible older sister. He was surprised at how delicate and vulnerable she actually looked. Why had he never noticed? More than ever, he wanted to protect her and care for her as she had always done for him. He wanted her to be able to relax and enjoy her life, knowing he'd be there for her.

"You want to go swing?" He gently put his arm through hers. "This time, I'll push."

6

a brother's
counsel

Cheer each other on to love and
good deeds! Encourage and
build each other up. Challenge
those who need to be inspired,
encourage the timid, and help the
weak. Demonstrate patience to
everyone. Make it your goal to
practice kindness to everyone.
Always be joyful. Pray continually.
And always give thanks to God!

Guiding you,
Your God of Wisdom

—from Hebrews 10:24; 1 Thessalonians 5:11, 14–18

Did you ever play the don't-answer-when-they-call-me game? You know, the one where your brother or sister calls your name, and you pretend you don't hear them until they're screaming. Finally, your mother intervenes and makes you answer.

I'm sure you did. But you only wanted a little peace and quiet, right? It seems your siblings always wanted to ask or tell you something. Your mother never could understand the game, but wasn't it fun to aggravate them just a little?

As the years passed, you realized you were glad when your siblings called your name, wanting advice on a business deal or just to tell you a bit of good news. Thinking back, your role as counselor was firmly set the first time your little brother or sister cried to you after a bike wreck or an insult from a classmate. You put your arm around them and assured them that everything would be OK. You told them how to fix the bike and how to handle a bully.

Now that you're older, your siblings still need your wise counsel. They depend on you to listen to them and speak words that will help, not harm, them. Even when you say something difficult or tough, it's because you love them.

It still isn't an easy job, being a brother. You question your own judgment sometimes— but they never do. A good brother is better than any professional counselor around.

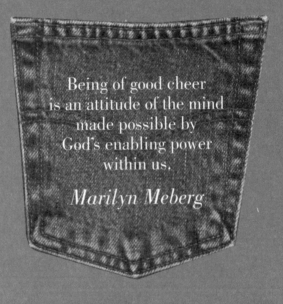

Being of good cheer
is an attitude of the mind
made possible by
God's enabling power
within us.

Marilyn Meberg

In spite of his excitement at leaving, part of him was unwilling to sleep away his last few hours at home. Tomorrow, everything would change forever.

The Greatest Cheerleader

The house was dark and quiet as Jared finished packing. The rest of the family had gone to bed hours ago, but Jared was clinging to the night. In spite of his excitement at leaving, part of him was unwilling to sleep away his last few hours at home. Tomorrow, everything would change forever.

He took in the sights, sounds, and smells of home with heightened awareness. The sound of the air-conditioner kicking on, the creaks the old hardwood floor made even when he tiptoed down the hall, the buzz of the refrigerator, and the tick-tick-tick of the grandfather clock—they'd all been part of his life for more than eighteen years. It was hard to say good-bye, no matter how ready he was for college.

It was after midnight, but Jared's mind was so full that he doubted he'd be able to sleep. *I'd better sleep,* he admonished himself. *Tomorrow's a big day.*

As he brushed his teeth, Jared walked to the family room to look at the trophies, awards, and family photos on display. He glanced at photos of his sister Darcy's college graduation, of his brother Steven grinning at the Eiffel Tower during his junior year abroad, and of his parents with a large, wedding-style cake at their twenty-fifth anniversary celebration last month. His gaze lingered on his own high-school graduation photo and one of his little sister, Angel, decked out in a baseball cap, ball glove, and team pennant at one of Jared's high-school baseball games.

There was Jared's all-state baseball championship trophy—and two for being his team's MVP. Even some of his Little-League trophies still stood on the shelf along with Darcy's basketball trophies and Steven's music-festival awards. But Jared was most proud of the medals six-year-old Angel had won at Special Olympics. Remembering her joy at competing brought a smile to his face. He had to throw his head back, thrust out his chin, and suck in to keep from drooling toothpaste onto his baseball-jersey pajamas.

As he ducked back into the bathroom to rinse his mouth, Jared heard something. He stood still and listened. Sure enough, muffled sobs came from Angel's bedroom. He wiped his mouth and went toward her room.

"Angel?" he asked quietly into the darkness. As his eyes adjusted to the dim light from her angel night-light, he could see his sister lying on her stomach; her head buried in her pillow. He sat on the bed next to her and gently turned her over to see her face. He wasn't surprised that she wore the baseball shirt from his new college team and was clutching the stuffed lion—his team's mascot—that he had given her as a going-away present.

He could feel that Angel's pillow was wet with tears, and her face was puffy and red from crying. She melted into Jared's arms and clung to him in a way that both warmed and broke his big-brother heart.

"What's wrong, sport? It's time for little girls to be sleeping—dreaming about having fun and playing baseball—not crying."

"I don't want you to go," she gasped between great sobs that wracked her body and made him hug her closer. "Stay here with me—always."

"Hey, I'll be with you always," he assured her kindly. "In here." He pointed to her heart and then to his.

"But I won't be able to play with you or talk to you," she protested. "Who'll show me how to slide home . . . or teach me how to run fast . . . or send me a signal when it's safe to steal second?"

"I'll still do all those things," Jared promised.

"But you'll be far away!"

"It's not that far away." Jared stroked her hair reassuringly. "You can come and visit me all the time, and I'll be home lots of weekends. You know you can call me anytime."

"But I'll miss watching your games." Angel stuck out her lower lip and twisted her chubby face into a pout.

"It's not baseball season yet," Jared said with a chuckle.

"But when it is, Mom and Dad will bring you to my home games. You can cheer for me just like always."

Angel's eyes welled up again with tears. "You won't know I'm there."

"Of course I will!" He wiped her eyes with his sleeve and kissed the top of her head. "Why wouldn't I know you're there?"

Angel was silent then grudgingly admitted her fear. "I saw . . ." Angel whispered. "I saw."

"What did you see?" Jared asked. She pointed to the brochure on the nightstand by her bed. It was one the athletic recruiters had left behind. It featured an impressive photo of the baseball stadium filled with thousands of screaming fans. Suddenly, Jared understood.

"It's a lot of people," Jared said knowingly. "But you'll still be my best cheerleader."

Angel nodded. "But you won't be able to hear me cheer."

"We'll use the special hand signals I taught you," Jared replied. "Thumbs up means swing for the fences, a finger on the nose means great job, and pulling on my ear means I hear you."

a brother's counsel

"And three fingers means I love you!" Angel piped up eagerly, touching her chest near her heart.

"That's right." Jared smiled. "See, you can still be my number-one cheerleader and fan."

"But so many people . . ." Angel struggled to put her thoughts into the right words. "You won't hear me."

"With the hand signals, I don't have to hear you," Jared comforted her. "I'll 'hear' you cheering with my eyes and in my heart."

"But how will you find me with so many people?" Angel demanded. "You won't have time to see me in the crowd before you bat."

"We'll work it out, sport." He tousled her hair then tucked her back under the covers. "Come to the game early, get a good seat before everyone else shows up, and then I'll know right where to look for you every time."

The answer seemed to satisfy Angel. She continued sniffling as she thought about that solution, but there were no more tears. "You're smart, Jared. You don't need to go to college to get smarter. Stay home with me."

"I may not need to get smarter," Jared joked, "but I need to go to college so I can play baseball."

Angel nodded with understanding. "I'll miss when you talk to me."

"I'll miss it too. Now go to sleep." He turned to go but stopped in the doorway. "I love you."

"Love you," Angel replied, yawning. She turned on her side and closed her eyes. Tomorrow she'd go with Jared to see his dorm and his new baseball field. That seemed to be enough.

◆

It was the home opener for the state college Lions. More than an hour before the game, while Jared and his teammates ran laps and took batting practice, he saw his parents and little sister claim their seats in the stands. Dressed head to toe in the gold and white colors of his team, Angel jumped up and down, waving excitedly. He waved back and touched three fingers to his heart: I love you! Across the distance he couldn't quite make it out, but he assumed she returned his signal.

a brother's counsel

"That's quite a cheerleader you have there," a teammate said with a chuckle. "She doesn't sit still for a minute."

"That's my little sister," Jared explained proudly. "She's my biggest fan."

Just before the game started, Jared saw his mother leading Angel out. *Probably going to the rest room or getting a hot dog,* Jared thought. *They'd better hurry back. I bat fourth.*

But when the game started, he hadn't seen them come back. By now the stands were so full he lost track of where they'd been sitting. He shaded his eyes with his hand and struggled in vain for a glimpse of his family, especially the little golden cheerleader.

His team went down one, two, three in their first at-bats. Not a great start, but at least it gave Mom and Angel more time to get back before he batted. He tried to concentrate on the game, but the puzzle about his missing cheering section distracted him. He was disappointed to think they might miss his first college at-bat.

When the bottom of the second rolled around, Jared strode slowly to the batter's box, still scanning the crowd.

He finally saw his dad, but his heart fell as he realized the seats next to him were empty.

Set it aside, he willed himself. *Concentrate on getting a hit.*

Jared looked down the third-base line for the coach's signal. He adjusted his glove, knocked dirt from his cleats, then stepped into the batter's box. Something beyond the pitcher caught Jared's eye. He raised his hand to call time and stepped out of the box. He looked toward the homerun zone, far out beyond the center-field fence. He could just make out a small figure dressed in gold jumping up and down and waving. Beside her was a giant sign with a bulls-eye. The sign read, "Hit it here, Jared."

With relief and satisfaction, Jared tugged on his ear with an exaggerated motion. Angel might not see it, but she'd know soon enough that he'd "heard." He stepped in and watched the ball sail hard and fast down the middle of the plate. Then he did exactly what his best cheerleader had requested.

Craaack!

7

a brother's
support

I am for you! I'm your refuge
and your strength . . . your ever-
present help in times of trouble.
Brothers were designed to come
alongside to help each other over
life's bumps. You can be confident
that I'll finish the good things I've
started in your life.

Blessings,
Your Ever-Faithful Provider

—from Romans 8:31; Psalm 46:1; Proverbs 17:17;
Philippians 1:6

Brothers come in all shapes and sizes. Sometimes they look alike. Other times no one would ever guess they're related. But one thing all brothers have in common is a bond that connects them more surely than any physical cords. No matter where we are, the bonds of brotherhood reach us at our point of need and give what we need most—support.

True brothers will always be there for each other. They're never too tired to go the extra mile. They're always ready to listen and share our dreams. True brothers are there when tragedy hits and will volunteer to do whatever is needed. They support us through the tough times and celebrate when we rejoice.

Being a brother means more than just having the same genes. Two men might be biologically unrelated yet still call each other brother. Athletes pat each other on the back and say, "Good job, brother!" When fraternity members pass on the college campus, they call out a greeting: "Hey, brother!" Pastors ask their church "brothers" to join them for special work days.

Just as houses need strong support systems to endure the devastating storms that are certain to come along from time to time, so do relationships. A brother is an important support beam that keeps the structure of a relationship solid because he's always willing, always able, always there. Thank you for the support you've given your friends and your family. You are truly worthy to be called brother.

The power of a
strong relationship
sustains us
and gives us strength.

Max Lucado

Brad wasn't stupid. He knew he had to get out. Before retreating, he grabbed the only thing within reach: his hunting rifle.

Band of Brothers

"Brad, the shop's on fire!" Marianne screamed to her husband sleeping beside her.

"No!" Brad yelled, jumping out of bed and running to the window to see for himself. Sure enough, smoke was coming from the workshop. "No . . . oh no!"

Brad shoved his feet into the worn slippers by his bed and raced for the door. He didn't even think of stopping to throw a bathrobe or coat over his pajamas to protect him from the damp chill of the November night air. He just knew he had to get to his beloved shop. If he could only get to it quickly enough, surely he could save it—save something—anything.

"I only see smoke," Brad told Marianne as she caught up to him outside the shop, carrying his bathrobe. "I'm going in to see what I can save."

"Oh, Brad, please don't go in," Marianne pleaded.

"I'll be all right," Brad assured her. "Maybe it's only a small fire, and we can put it out ourselves." He put his hand on the door. It didn't feel too hot. "You get the hose while I try to bring things out." But when he opened the door, the draft of air only fueled the fire, sending flames shooting up to the ceiling.

Brad wasn't stupid. He knew he had to get out. Before closing the door and retreating, he grabbed the only thing within reach: his hunting rifle. It was the only thing that belonged in the shop to survive the fire—except for Brad.

He and Marianne retreated from the fire's heat. They crouched on the ground twenty feet from the shop and watched as flames escaped from the windows and engulfed the building.

Brad vaguely realized he was trembling. His eyes felt seared and his face tight and hot from the heat, but it barely registered. The magnitude of his loss consumed him as the fire consumed his shop. "All my tools . . ." Brad mumbled, shaking his head in shocked disbelief. "Doris's entertainment center . . ."

"Oh, Brad," Marianne commiserated. "You had just finished it, and now your sister will never even get to see it." She put her arm supportively around Brad's waist and wiped a tear from her sooty cheek. "You worked so hard on it. It was beautiful."

True to Brad's nature, he had been meticulous right up to the last stroke of varnish. He had proudly showed off the finished project to Marianne earlier that evening. Then, with great pride and delight, Brad had called his sister to announce that the masterpiece was done. She had sounded excited and said she couldn't wait to see it. But always wanting to help, Brad had volunteered to deliver the piece the next morning. That way she'd have time to make room for the new piece and wouldn't have to go looking for someone to help her move it. After all, there was no hurry. It wasn't going anywhere.

And now it never would. Brad stood with his arm around Marianne as he watched his labor of love for his sister be reduced to a pile of ashes.

Soon big red fire engines came racing down the street and up the driveway. They pumped many gallons of water trying to tame the beastly fire, but it was too late. The shop and its contents were a total loss.

Brad's mind and body felt numb. In a daze he watched the fire trucks' flashing red lights reflect off the puddles of water surrounding the smoldering remains of his precious memories. Even after the fire was out, the last firefighters had left, and Marianne had gone back inside to get clean and warm, Brad wouldn't think of going inside.

An hour later, when the sun came up, Brad still stood by the ashes, wiping away a tear or two, smiling now and then as he reminisced about the golden hours spent in the shop— the many gifts of love he'd created there.

He'd built the shop himself. A carpenter by trade, Brad had used the three-thousand-square-foot workshop as his place of business. Then, though successful and in demand, he had chosen to retire early so he could work on the projects he enjoyed most—using his hands and his heart to help and bless others. He'd made Marianne's beloved dining-room table and chairs in this shop. Deep within him, Brad felt the first stirrings of gratitude. Thank God the fire hadn't spread to the house—the beautiful home he'd built for his bride forty-two years ago.

He breathed a sigh of relief. The house was full of projects Brad had made in the shop. Each one held another memory the fire hadn't managed to steal. Soon his mind embraced a broader, more comforting truth. The fruits of his labor were not all destroyed in the blaze; they were scattered abroad in the homes, the hearts, and the lives of the many people he loved. His newly married daughter's home was graced by kitchen cabinets he'd made. His granddaughter had a playhouse that made her the most popular little girl in the neighborhood, and his grandsons had a tree house that would always bear Brad's signature of craftsmanship and love. Several babies at church slept each night in beautifully ornate cribs thanks to Brad's generosity and artistry.

a brother's support

But Brad had built more than furniture in his workshop. He'd built relationships. He'd been born with four brothers, but through the years he'd collected a great many more. "How are you doing, brother?" was the typical way Brad greeted the men he befriended. And Brad befriended everyone with open arms and brotherly love.

He had developed a reputation as someone with a listening ear for any brother in trouble. Men gravitated to him for sound advice and wise counsel. Tuesday evenings in the shop had always been reserved for Brad's Overcomers group. As he taught them to build things with their hands, he helped men struggling with addictions rebuild their lives.

On Sunday nights another group of brothers would invade the shop for fellowship. Yet another set joined Brad to discuss ways to be better husbands, better fathers, and better men.

And on any given morning, before the sun rose above the hills, Brad loved to see two or three trucks winding down the country road to his house. He greeted each brother with a pot of coffee, a welcoming smile, and a scripture or two to challenge their hearts.

Brad grieved the loss of his shop—the fine collection of the latest tools as well as some cherished antiques he'd collected through the years. He felt the ache of losing "friends," half-finished projects, plans for new starts, and Doris's undelivered home entertainment center. But even in grief, his heart welled up in thanksgiving. He'd truly been blessed—and been a blessing—through his shop. The memories, the furniture he'd crafted, and the lives he'd helped build were the workshop's greatest legacy. It was a legacy that made him proud.

Word of the night's events spread as fast as the fire itself, and one by one Brad's family and friends filled his yard to offer support. This time it was Brad who enjoyed the hugs, encouragement, and love from his many brothers who came to help. Someone brought coffee. Another, doughnuts. One was Brad's insurance agent, another his pastor.

"Anything we can do to help?" each man asked in turn.

"No," Brad told them with a grateful smile. "Insurance will cover the loss. It's just too bad that the new stuff won't have the same sentimental memories as the old ones. Each tool, each scrap of wood had its own unique story—mostly associated with a project I made with or for someone special." He toed the soggy ground with his muddy slipper. "I guess that's something you just can't get back."

By the weekend Brad had finished clearing the remains of the shop from his property. It was Sunday morning, late in November, when hearts and minds are naturally turned toward Thanksgiving. But it wouldn't have mattered what month it was. It was time to honor a friend and brother in a unique way. That morning at church, blood brothers and spiritual brothers came together as one. Their heritage and last names didn't matter; they shared the most important bond—a bond of the heart.

One by one the brothers came and laid at Brad's feet the tools of his life's work. One brought a hammer, one a saw, another a sander or a drill—each symbolic of the work Brad loved but more importantly a symbol of their love and respect for Brad.

The carpenter didn't even attempt to hide his tears at the unexpected outpouring of brotherly love. He knew that even without the workshop, he was still building something of value with his brothers—something no fire could ever destroy.

You are only as strong as your purpose; therefore, let us choose reasons to act that are big, bold, righteous, and eternal.

Barry Munro